SABRINA FISHER REECE

Sexuality & Spirituality

Unlocking the Sacred Power Between Body and Soul

This book is dedicated to anyone who has ever loved deeply, lost painfully, or found themselves bound to someone their soul was never meant to stay with.

To those who have questioned the intensity of their emotions, the pull of their desires, or the mystery of connections that didn't make sense.

To every heart that has broken, healed, opened again, and dared to search for meaning in the spaces between pleasure and pain, passion and purpose. I pray this book brings you peace

Love Bri Reece

Contents

1

The Sacred Bridge Between Body and Soul

Most people grow up believing their spiritual life exists "up there," somewhere in the heavens, while their physical life stays "down here," tied to flesh, desire, and human weakness. Many of us who were raised in the church were taught that sexual feelings were sinful, shameful, or something to avoid until marriage — as if our bodies and our spirits lived in two separate worlds. But that separation was never God's intention. The body was never created to be the enemy of the spirit; it was created as a vessel to express the spirit. Beautiful intimacy is not something to fear, hide, or be ashamed of — it is something to understand, honor, and experience with the right heart, the right energy, and the right alignment.

Your soul did not come to Earth to avoid the body. Your soul came to Earth *through* the body. The body is the bridge — the sacred, divine bridge — between the invisible and the physical, between heaven and earth. Without it, you could not experience growth, connection, touch, healing, intimacy, or awakening.

Your experiences help your soul evolve.

When you begin to understand this, your entire relationship with yourself begins to shift. You stop fighting the very vessel God gave you. You stop separating your desires from your divinity. You stop feeling guilty for being human — and you begin to see how being human is its own sacred spiritual initiation.

Your Body Is the Soul's First Language

Your soul speaks to you constantly, but it doesn't speak in words first — it speaks through sensations.

Before you "think" anything, your body already knows.

Your heart tightens around danger before your mind can explain it.

Your stomach drops when you are out of alignment.

Your chest warms when you are around someone safe.

Your breath slows when your spirit recognizes peace.

Your skin tingles when you meet someone who mirrors your own soul.

And your body awakens with desire long before a single touch — because attraction, too, is a form of truth.

Words come second. The body speaks first. This is why ignoring your body is the fastest way to disconnect from your spiritual truth. And listening to your body is the fastest way to reconnect with it. Your body feels everything the soul already knows.

Why So Many People Feel Divided

Most people were taught to split themselves down the middle: the spiritual self over here, the physical self over there. They learned:

- "Don't trust your feelings."
- "Ignore your desires."
- Repress any sexual thoughts or feelings
- "Your body is a temptation."
- "Spirituality requires denial."

But separation always creates suffering. Whenever you exile any part of yourself — your sensuality, your desires, your needs, your feelings — you exile *a piece of your soul* with it. The disconnection doesn't bring you closer to God; it brings you farther from yourself.

Spirituality is not the rejection of the physical. Spirituality is the *integration* of it. Your soul chose your body for a reason.

The Divine Intelligence Within the Body

Every part of your body carries wisdom.

Your nervous system is wired with divine intelligence.

Your intuition is embedded in your cells.

Your emotions are spiritual messengers.

Your hormones carry energetic messages.

Your desire is a compass pointing toward growth.

Your pleasure is a doorway to presence and awakening.

And your sexuality — that sacred, creative fire — is the same energy God used to form universes. It is not dirty. It is not sinful. It is not shameful. It's time to release that old belief.

Understanding your sexuality is powerful. It is creation. It is healing. It is truth. Sexual energy is spiritual energy in motion. The only reason people fear it is because they were taught to suppress what they never learned to understand. We instill that fear in children from the beginning of their lives, teaching them boundaries through shame instead of wisdom.

But the body is beautiful. The body is divine. And none of us would exist without the very energy we were taught to hide.

I wrote this book because I remember being young, raised in the Christian church, and conditioned to believe that any physical desire was wrong or from the Devil. Yet at the same time, I remember kids in that same church sneaking kisses in closets — and a few even becoming pregnant.

I understand completely why no parent wants their 13-year-old daughter to end up in that situation. But maybe if the subject hadn't been avoided, if we weren't taught to fear our bodies or bury our questions, young people would've known the consequences, understood their own feelings, and felt safer communicating with the adults in their lives.

Desire Is Not the Enemy — Disconnection Is

Desire becomes destructive only when it is disconnected from the soul.

But when aligned with your inner truth, desire becomes holy. Your desire reveals:

- what you crave emotionally,
- what you long for spiritually,

4

- what your soul is ready for,
- what your body is tired of tolerating,
- what kind of connection you're truly built for.

In this way, desire acts as a spiritual compass, guiding you toward people, experiences, and lessons that will grow you.

Your soul uses desire to get your attention.

This is why some connections feel magnetic — you're not imagining it. Souls recognize each other long before bodies speak or touch. When you encounter a soul you are meant to learn from, heal with, or grow with, you feel it.

It's a pull. A knowing. A familiarity.

A vibration that speaks louder than logic.

Your Body Stores Your Spiritual History

Your body carries everything your soul has been through.

It stores:

- unspoken grief,
- unresolved trauma,
- childhood wounds,
- broken promises,
- spiritual awakenings,
- sacred connections,
- sexual memories,
- moments of shame,
- moments of holiness.

Your body remembers what your mind tries to forget. This is why healing isn't just mental. Healing is physical. Healing is cellular. Healing is energetic. Healing is spiritual. When you heal the body, you heal the story. When you heal the story, you free the soul. The more you release what's stored in your body, the clearer your spiritual connection becomes.

Presence: The Ritual of Returning Home to Yourself

The sacred bridge between body and soul strengthens through presence.

Presence is the moment you stop running.

Stop numbing.

Stop separating.

Stop shaming.

Stop suppressing.

Presence is when you return to the truth of what you feel.

Presence is when you listen to your body with compassion instead of judgment.

Presence is when you allow your emotions to move instead of burying them.

In presence, the body softens and the soul rises.

You become more intuitive.

More grounded.

More connected.

More magnetic.

More spiritually aligned.

More deeply yourself.

Presence is the true beginning of spiritual intimacy — first with yourself, then with others.

When the Body and Soul Unite, You Become Whole

When the physical and the spiritual stop fighting each other, you become powerful:

- You stop choosing partners out of loneliness.
- You stop betraying yourself to be loved.
- You stop ignoring your needs.
- You stop shrinking your desires.
- You stop living from wounds.
- You start living from purpose.

This inner union — this marriage of body and soul — is the foundation of sacred sexuality and divine connection.

Before you can merge with another soul, you must learn to merge with your own.

Before you can love another deeply, you must learn to inhabit your own body fully.

Before you can surrender to intimacy, you must feel safe inside yourself.

This is the sacred bridge.

This is where true spirituality begins.

Inside you.

Your body is not the barrier to your spiritual evolution — it is the portal.

And walking across that bridge will change everything.

2

Energetic Exchange: What Really Happens During Intimacy

A lot people think intimacy is simply a physical act — two bodies coming together, sharing a moment, a spark, a release. But what they rarely understand is that intimacy is far more spiritual than it is physical. The body participates in the experience, yes, but the soul is the one doing the real work. The soul is the one absorbing, exchanging, receiving, giving, merging, and remembering.

Every intimate experience leaves an energetic fingerprint and that fingerprint doesn't disappear just because the moment ends. Intimacy is not casual. Connection is not casual. Touch is not casual. Energy is not casual.

The moment two bodies come together, two entire universes collide — not just flesh to flesh, but spirit to spirit, story to story, lifetime to lifetime. Every person carries histories, traumas, desires, wounds, prayers, dreams, fears, memories, and frequencies. And when intimacy happens, those energies don't just touch — they merge.

The body may forget quickly, but the energy never does. The spirit archives every exchange: the truth of the connection, the intention behind it, the emotional weight within it. That's why you can walk away from someone and still feel them. Why their presence lingers in your chest, your mood, your thoughts, your dreams. Energy makes an imprint that the mind cannot erase.

This is why intimacy transforms you, even when you pretend it doesn't. It shifts your vibration, your clarity, your confidence, your peace. Sometimes it elevates you. Sometimes it drains you. But it always leaves a mark.

And it's not just women who feel this. Men feel it too — deeply. They just weren't raised to speak about it. Ego becomes the armor that hides their spiritual sensitivity. But their spirit knows when it has touched something divine, and it knows when it has absorbed something heavy. Their energy remembers just as much as ours does.

Intimacy is never just physical. It is a sacred exchange — a blending of frequencies, a sharing of spiritual information, a moment where two souls intertwine. No one walks away the same. Whether they acknowledge it or not, every encounter writes something new into their spirit.

Your Body Doesn't Just Connect — Your Energy Does

Have you ever noticed that after being intimate with someone:

- you start thinking their thoughts,
- feeling their emotions,
- dreaming their dreams,
- craving what they crave,
- carrying their stress or sadness,

· losing your clarity or gaining new clarity?

That is not imagination. That is **energetic merging**. The soul absorbs more than the body: When you lie with someone, your body intertwines, but your energy entangles. Your fields overlap. Your spirit opens. Your intuition softens. Your heart becomes porous.

For a moment — sometimes for months, sometimes forever — your frequencies become one. Intimacy is the closest thing we have to spiritual fusion.

This is why you can be intimate with someone you're not "supposed" to care about and still feel deeply bonded. This is why you can miss someone who wasn't good for you. This is why breakups feel like withdrawals. This is why "just sex" is never "just sex." Your soul knows what your mind denies.

Soul Imprints: The Energetic Marks We Leave on Each Other

Every person you connect with leaves an imprint — a residue of their energy — on your heart, your nervous system, and your aura.

This imprint can show up as:

· unexplained sadness,
· sudden insecurities,
· deep comfort,
· heightened intuition,
· confidence,
· motivation,
· confusion,

- anxiety,
- desire,
- or healing.

It depends on the energy of the person you joined with. Some people lighten your spirit simply by touching you. Others drain your spirit even when they hold you. Energy is not neutral. It is either nourishing you or weakening you. Your job is to learn the difference.

Why Some People Feel Addictive

The most intense connections are not always healthy — but they are always energetic.

You feel addicted to someone because:

- they awaken a dormant part of your soul,
- your trauma recognizes their trauma,
- your frequency matches theirs,
- your body craves the familiar,
- your chemistry responds to their energy,
- the intimacy activated spiritual lessons you didn't know you needed.

Your body becomes addicted to the feeling.

Your nervous system becomes addicted to the pattern.

Your soul becomes addicted to the purpose.

Sometimes the purpose is healing.

Sometimes the purpose is awakening.

Sometimes the purpose is ending a cycle.

Sometimes the purpose is preparing you for real love.

Sometimes the purpose is remembering yourself.
But it is *never* random.

Sex Is Not Just Physical — It's a Transfer of Power

When you open your body to someone, you open your energetic gates:

- your heart chakra,
- your sacral chakra,
- your root chakra,
- your aura,
- your emotional field.

You allow someone to step inside your spiritual house. Every touch, every moan, every breath, every release — all of it is an invocation of energy. You are pulling them into your field while they pull you into theirs.

This is why:

- you must be careful who you give access to,
- you feel tired after intimacy with the wrong person,
- you feel energized after intimacy with the right one,
- you can lose yourself in someone,
- you can find yourself in someone,
- you can be spiritually elevated or spiritually drained.

You can have a healthy, aligned sexual connection that makes you glow...Or you can have a toxic, unaligned sexual connection that empties your spirit. Both are intimacy. But only one is sacred.

What You Absorb from Someone During Intimacy

Energetic exchange during intimacy can include:

1. Emotional Energy

Their stress, anger, joy, trauma, and mood can transfer into you.

2. Mental Energy

Their thoughts, beliefs, and mindset can influence yours.

3. Spiritual Energy

Their wounds, their shadows, their lessons, their light.

4. Ancestral Energy

Generational patterns and inherited vibrations.

5. Soul Energy

Desire, purpose, intention, identity.

6. Physical Energy

Hormonal and nervous system activation.
This is why after intimacy you may feel:

- lighter,
- confused,
- angry,
- inspired,
- numb,
- spiritually open,
- spiritually disconnected.

What you absorbed determines how you feel.

This is not magic — it is energetic law.

Your Aura Remembers Every Connection

The aura — your energetic field — holds the imprint of every intimate partner you've ever had. Some imprints fade quickly. Others linger for years. The deeper the intimacy, the deeper the imprint. This is why you can still feel someone long after they leave. This is why you can sense when someone is thinking about you. This is why certain people never fully detach until you spiritually release them. This is why some connections feel like they live in your bones. Energy stays until you consciously let it go.

The Soul Knows When Intimacy Is Aligned

Aligned intimacy feels like:

- safety
- peace
- clarity
- expansion

- presence
- connection
- surrender
- awakening

Unaligned intimacy feels like:

- emptiness
- confusion
- guilt
- anxiety
- disconnection
- doubt
- self-abandonment

The body knows.
   The soul knows.
   Your energy knows.
   Trust the knowing.

There Is No Such Thing as Casual Connection

The idea of "casual" intimacy only works when the heart is numb, the body is disconnected, and the soul is ignored. But once you awaken — once you begin living consciously — you realize:
   Every kiss is an exchange.
   Every touch is a language.
   Every breath is an offering.
   Every moment is a connection.
   Every connection is spiritual.

Every spiritual connection has purpose.

Your body is divine.

Your energy is holy.

Your intimacy is sacred.

What you share with someone is not small — it is powerful.

Intimacy Is the Meeting Place of Souls

When two people come together with purity, intention, and alignment, intimacy becomes a prayer. A meditation. A healing ceremony. A merging of energies that opens portals inside both people. This type of intimacy: raises your vibration, awakens your spirit, balances your energies, clears your mind, softens your heart, softens your heart, elevates your consciousness.

It becomes a spiritual experience disguised as a physical one. This is what sacred sexuality looks like. This is what divine union feels like. This is what true intimacy is meant to be. Two bodies, two energies, two souls but one frequency.

The Responsibility of Intimacy

When you understand the truth about energetic exchange, you stop:

- giving your body to people who can't hold your heart,
- sharing your energy with people who drain your spirit,
- confusing lust with alignment,
- settling for connection without purpose,
- ignoring your body's signals,
- abandoning your intuition.

You start:

- choosing consciously,
- protecting your peace,
- honoring your body,
- respecting your energy,
- listening to your soul,
- connecting with intention,
- healing before merging,
- loving from alignment rather than loneliness.

This is the difference between ordinary sex and sacred union. Ordinary sex touches the body. Sacred union transforms the soul.

You Are Worth Sacred Connection

Your intimacy is not cheap and your energy is not free. Your body is not a possession and our soul is not a playground. Your spirit is not a casual experience and you are a portal. You are a healer. You are a universe. You are divine energy in human form.

And when you begin to honor the sacredness of your own intimacy — no matter who you love, how you love, or what your orientation may be — you naturally invite partners who honor the sacredness within you.

Because everything shifts the moment you stop reaching for connection from a place of emptiness... and begin choosing intimacy from a place of wholeness. This is the true power of energetic exchange: two souls meeting with intention, respect, and truth.

This is what happens when sexuality and spirituality rise together instead of being forced apart. This is the beauty of letting yourself feel, desire, and express without shame. Most people go their entire lives without discovering this simple truth: your intimacy is not just physical — it is Divine and when you honor it, the universe sends you someone who honors it too.

3

Emotional Intimacy vs. Spiritual Intimacy

Most people confuse emotional intimacy with spiritual intimacy. They assume that if they can talk to someone for hours, open up about their past, cry together, or share vulnerable moments, then they must be deeply connected.

But emotional intimacy and spiritual intimacy are not the same.One opens the heart. The other opens the soul. One makes you feel safe. The other makes you feel seen. One helps you heal. The other helps you evolve. Emotional intimacy is human. Spiritual intimacy is divine.

Both are powerful — but they do not operate on the same level. And until you learn the difference, you may mistake emotional closeness for spiritual purpose, or confuse spiritual connection with emotional attachment. Understanding these two forms of intimacy will completely reshape how you choose partners, how you connect, and how you protect your energy.

Emotional Intimacy: The Human Connection

Emotional intimacy is the comfort of being known. It is built through conversation, vulnerability, shared experiences, honesty, and trust. Emotional intimacy feels like:

- "I can be myself with you."
- "I feel safe telling you the truth."
- "You understand my pain."
- "You make my heart soften."

Emotional intimacy often shows up as:

- long conversations,
- deep confessions,
- shared childhood stories,
- mutual comfort,
- bonding through trauma,
- mutual empathy.

It is healing. It is nurturing. It is affirming. It can be very beautiful. But emotional intimacy alone does not mean you are spiritually aligned with someone. Many people mistake emotional comfort for spiritual compatibility. Just because someone can hold your heart does not mean they can hold your soul.

The Limitations of Emotional Intimacy

Emotional intimacy can make you feel close to someone who:

- is not aligned with your purpose,
- cannot grow with you,
- is emotionally dependent,
- mirrors your unhealed wounds,
- or feeds parts of you that are still hurting.

Sometimes emotional intimacy feels like love... when in reality, it's trauma bonding. Sometimes it feels like connection...when it's actually emotional familiarity. Sometimes it feels like "home"... but the only reason it feels like home is because it resembles your past. Emotional intimacy can soothe you — even when the relationship is not meant to last. This is why emotional intimacy alone cannot sustain spiritual growth.

Spiritual Intimacy: The Soul Connection

Spiritual intimacy is not built through conversation — it is built through presence. It is the merging of energy, the meeting of consciousness, the recognition of a shared frequency. You don't talk your way into spiritual intimacy; you feel your way into it.

Spiritual intimacy feels like:

- "My soul remembers you."
- "I grow when I'm connected to you."
- "You activate something inside me."
- "Being with you elevates my vibration."

Where emotional intimacy is comforting, spiritual intimacy is **awakening**. Where emotional intimacy makes you feel safe, spiritual intimacy makes you feel **expanded**.Where emotional intimacy bonds your heart, spiritual intimacy activates your **purpose**.Spiritual intimacy challenges you, stretches you, transforms you. It is not about emotional comfort — it is about spiritual evolution.

The Signs of Spiritual Intimacy

You know a connection is spiritually intimate when:

1. You grow spiritually in their presence

Their energy awakens dormant parts of you.
   You become more conscious, more intuitive, more self-aware.

2. Your intuition speaks louder

You feel guided, aligned, and connected to your inner wisdom.

3. The connection feels bigger than physical attraction

It's not about the body — it's about the soul recognizing itself.

4. Your vibration rises around them

You feel more alive, more joyful, more powerful, more YOU.

5. The connection exposes your shadows

Not to break you, but to evolve you.

6. Your energy merges naturally

There is no force, no fear — only flow.

7. The bond feels timeless

You feel like you've known them before you ever met.

Why People Confuse the Two

Emotional intimacy often feels like love because it satisfies the heart's need for closeness. Spiritual intimacy often feels intense because it satisfies the soul's need for truth. Most relationships begin emotionally. But the ones that become divine — the ones that feel destined — begin spiritually. When you experience both in the same person, the connection becomes transformative. But when you only experience one, it creates imbalance. Emotional intimacy without spiritual intimacy can feel:

- safe but stagnant,
- comforting but unfulfilling,
- close but not aligned.

Spiritual intimacy without emotional intimacy can feel:

- magnetic but unstable,
- destined but overwhelming,

- powerful but confusing.

True sacred connection requires both.

The Most Dangerous Confusion: Emotional Closeness as "Soulmate Energy"

Many people fall in love with someone emotionally compatible and call it destiny. But emotional compatibility is not the same as soul alignment. You can share trauma, history, and vulnerability with someone and still not be aligned with them spiritually.

You can love someone emotionally and still know they cannot follow you into your next level. You can feel bonded to someone emotionally who your spirit keeps telling you to release. Emotional intimacy can feel like love. Spiritual intimacy feels like purpose.

How Emotional Intimacy Heals — But Spiritual Intimacy Transforms

Emotional intimacy helps you recover.
Spiritual intimacy helps you remember.
Emotional intimacy helps you feel safe.
Spiritual intimacy helps you become powerful.
Emotional intimacy helps you feel loved.
Spiritual intimacy helps you rise.
Emotional intimacy helps you process your past.
Spiritual intimacy helps you create your future.
You need both — but you must learn which one you're experiencing

so you don't assign meaning where there is only comfort.

When Emotional and Spiritual Intimacy Meet

This is where sacred union is born.
A relationship becomes divine when:

- your hearts feel safe,
- your souls feel seen,
- your spirits feel aligned,
- your bodies feel connected,
- your energy feels elevated.

This is the kind of connection that elevates your life,
awakens your purpose,
expands your consciousness,
and holds you through your evolution.
This is not common.
This is not casual.
This is not accidental.
This is divine orchestration.
This is spiritual partnership.
This is sacred intimacy.

Choosing From the Soul, Not the Wound

When you learn the difference between emotional and spiritual intimacy:

- you stop mistaking comfort for destiny,
- you stop attaching to the familiar,

- you stop ignoring your intuition,
- you stop forcing connections,
- you stop choosing from loneliness,
- you stop settling for "almost."

You begin choosing with clarity — not craving.
  With intuition — not fear.
  With alignment — not attachment.
  With purpose — not desperation.
  You begin choosing from your spirit and not your wounds.
  And that is when everything changes.

The Connection You Seek Is Seeking You

Somewhere in this world — or in the spiritual realm preparing to enter your life — is a person whose soul is aligned with yours. Someone who will meet you emotionally and spiritually. Someone who is safe enough for your heart and expansive enough for your spirit. Someone who feels like home but also feels like growth. When emotional intimacy meets spiritual intimacy, love becomes sacred, and so do you.

The truth is, many of us have lived most of our lives starving for a love we didn't know how to name. Wanting someone who could meet our hearts without wounding them, and meet our souls without fearing them. We've tried to build relationships from emotional need, hoping that closeness would turn into destiny — only to learn that emotional comfort can soothe the heart, but it cannot feed the soul.

There comes a moment in every person's life when they realize they can no longer pretend they don't feel what they feel. They can't force connections that drain them, and they can't ignore connections that awaken them. The soul reaches a point where it refuses to settle for anything less than truth. And that truth is simple: **your spirit knows what it needs, even when your heart is afraid to accept it.**

Emotional intimacy alone will make you feel held, but spiritual intimacy will make you feel whole. Emotional intimacy teaches you how to be vulnerable, but spiritual intimacy teaches you how to be free. When someone reaches you on a soul level, something inside you recognizes itself — a remembering, not a learning. It feels like God whispering, *"This is who you are when you stop shrinking."*

If you have ever cried over a relationship that felt safe but not aligned, or mourned a connection that was spiritually powerful but emotionally unstable, know this: you were never wrong for feeling deeply. You were never foolish for hoping. You were not naïve for believing there was more. You were simply awakening to the difference between being emotionally understood and spiritually seen.

And the moment you learn that difference, you stop chasing the kind of connection that only occupies your loneliness... and you start preparing for the kind of connection that elevates your life.

Somewhere, there is a soul whose energy will feel like oxygen. Someone who will speak to your heart *and* your spirit. Someone who expands you, challenges you, softens you, awakens you, and meets you in the places you thought no one could reach.

When emotional intimacy finally meets spiritual intimacy, love becomes more than a relationship — it becomes transformation. And the deepest truth of all is this:

You deserve that kind of love. You were born for that kind of intimacy, and when the time is right, it will find you — **because it already knows your name.**

4

How to Attract a Spiritually Aligned Partner

Growing up in the church, sexuality was something I was trained to fear, avoid, and silence. Church kids don't get the freedom to explore themselves the way others do. We were raised to believe that every desire was sinful, every thought was wrong, and anything happening before marriage was punishable by "fire and brimstone." So instead of learning about our bodies, we learned shame. Instead of discovering our sensuality, we learned suppression. Instead of being taught that sexuality is one of God's natural gifts, we were taught to fear it.

It took me until my forties — after years of studying spiritual truth and unlearning religious fear — to finally understand that sexuality is not separate from spirituality. They are intertwined. Deeply. Naturally. Divinely.

No one ever told me that intimacy carries spiritual weight. No one told me that sharing your body means exchanging energy. No one taught me that sex is not just physical — it is emotional, mental, and spiritual. So, like many people who grew up under religious pressure, I stepped into adulthood spiritually awakened but sexually uninformed. I participated in sex for the act alone, not realizing there is a **spiritual exchange** that happens every single time two people come together. We don't just share our bodies — we share our frequency, our trauma, our emotions, our minds, our shadows, our wounds, our desires, and our souls. And once I began my spiritual journey, things shifted.

Suddenly, the more awakened I became, the more connected I felt to my own sexuality. My mind, my body, and my spirit were no longer separate parts — they were communicating, harmonizing, and awakening together. My sexual urges weren't random; they were tied to my consciousness. My desire for deeper intimacy wasn't lust — it was spiritual hunger.

It took years before I could even speak about it. But as I continued reading book after book, attending lecture after lecture, and searching for truth through spiritual teachers like Joseph Murphy, Eckhart Tolle, Ernest Holmes, Don Miguel Ruiz, Neville Goddard, and Earl Nightingale, I began to see a pattern: **The more spiritually awake I became, the more sexually alive I became.**

Not in a promiscuous way — but in a conscious way. I started noticing something strange: Whenever I read a passage or sentence that felt like divine truth, my entire body would react — emotionally, spiritually, and even sexually. I felt awakened in a way that was impossible to ignore. I didn't understand it until I finally confided in a friend who had lived many lives — street hustler, preacher, teacher. He told me something that stayed with me forever:

"Sexuality and spirituality are connected. They always have been."

Once I embraced that truth, everything began to make sense. Why certain people felt magnetic. Why certain connections felt addictive. Why certain relationships were impossible to shake. Why my soul recognized people long before my mind did. And this leads me to one of the most powerful, painful, transformative lessons of my life — **my connection with D'Ablo.**

The Truth About Soul Ties, Attraction, and Misalignment

There are only a few men I have ever truly loved, and among them, my relationship with my youngest daughter's father — Phillip, known as D'Ablo   was the most passionate and spiritually complicated. From the very beginning, the connection was intense, addictive, magnetic, and at times, destructive.

For years, I told myself our chemistry was the problem. But now I know the truth: We had a soul tie — a deep, spiritual bond formed through intense emotional and physical connection, but not aligned for long-term partnership. The spiritual lesson came later. Looking back, I realize we were connected because we shared similar wounds. Both of us grew up feeling neglected. Both of us longed for love. Both of us wanted safety we didn't know how to ask for. Both of us carried childhood trauma that shaped our adult choices.Our souls recognized each other's pain, not each other's purpose and so began a cycle.

Years of passion, desire, arguments, reconnection, distance,

31

and return. Years of trying to love someone who wasn't capable of loving me the way I deserved. Years of hoping his tenderness would someday match his intensity. But even when the relationship failed emotionally, the sexual connection remained powerful... almost unbreakable. We coul dnot be in the same room very long without having sex.

We could be angry, disappointed, hurt, or done — and somehow, on look, one smile, one touch would ignite everything. It was as if our bodies remembered something our minds tried to forget. That type of physical connection is rare. But rare does not always mean right.

As I grew spiritually — studying manifestation, vibration, and divine truth — my desire for deeper connection grew too. I wanted conversations about purpose and destiny. I wanted growth. I wanted elevation. I wanted a partner whose mind stimulated me and whose spirit aligned with mine.

But D'Ablo wasn't evolving with me. No matter how much I hoped, prayed, or visualized, he remained emotionally guarded, controlling, inconsistent, and deeply shaped by his past. I kept seeing and hoping for what he *could* become instead of accepting who he was.

That's how soul ties work — they show you potential, not purpose. I thought compassion would change him. I thought the love for our baby girl would change him, I thought patience would soften him. I thought my love would inspire him. But love cannot force someone to do the work you're doing. And while I was walking toward healing, he was standing still.

The Vision That Changed Everything

The night everything shifted, I had just been intimate with him again. I felt bad about it because he had not seen our daughter for nine months. When it was over, instead of feeling fulfilled or connected, I felt unsettled. Sad. Spiritually conflicted. My soul felt disturbed, not soothed. I never felt comfortable telling him no.

Later that night, I experienced a "vision" — or spiritual encounter — that forever changed the way I saw him, myself, and the truth about spiritual alignment. This is what happened:

One evening, after once again engaging in my sexual relationship with my youngest daughter's father, I was emotionally upset because I felt, once again, that I was wasting valuable time on a man I simply had emotionally evolved past. A man whose battle scars ran too deep and whose unwillingness to grow emotionally caused my level of respect for him to greatly diminish. So, unlike other times when we had rekindled our intense sexual relationship, this time was different. I felt that the choice to do so was distracting me from my spiritual path, and my soul was visibly upset by my choice. I believed our sexual attraction was an unhealthy distraction. I took my daughters to eat shortly after the encounter and my baby girl who is his daughter as well, was five years old at the time, she kept asking me "Mommy what's wrong, why are you so sad?" I couldn't explain it, nor could I shake the feeling that I had. I tried to rationalize it in my mind by asking myself, "SaBrina, what's the big deal? You have slept with this man hundreds of times. Stop tripping." My entire soul seemed unsettled and disturbed. When I got home, I simply wanted to sleep it off, so I took a TylenolPM and had a glass of wine. That night something unexplainable happened.

As I slept, I was awakened by some sort of spiritual vision. Please understand that for sake of communication I will call it a vision, but I honestly do not know what it actually was. I am positive I was not asleep. In the vision, my daughter's father Phill (D'Ablo) got up out of bed. I was still lying there on the right side of the bed. He turned towards me. He had on a light blue shirt and light blue pants. Directly out of his clothing, down where his genital area was, a substance began to flow out of him and towards me. It flowed out consistently like water flowing from a hose. He turned towards the door as if he was leaving the room, but he seemed to be struggling to get there. He appeared to be moving in slow motion as if he had heavy weights on his feet. It took him so long to get to the door that I fell asleep, which is why I am certain that it was not a dream.

Apparently in his struggle to make it to the door he had fallen back onto the bed with me and we both had fallen asleep. I know that we both had indeed fallen asleep because It was the sound of his snoring that woke the both of us up and started this unusual spiritual interaction rolling again. Please understand, he was not physically present in the room. He was not in the house. This imagery that I was currently involved in was not actually happening in the physical, tangible sense. When we woke up, I noticed he was still in the room and had fallen back onto the bed and fallen asleep a third time. I said, "I thought you left." This spiritual him never spoke a word. I say the spiritual him because I am aware this moment was not actually happening in real time, but his body was not translucent or ghost-like. He appeared to be solid. He got back up and headed for the door attempting to leave again. He was still moving in very slow motion, literally struggling to make it to the door as if something was pulling him back. This time he actually made it to the door. His journey towards the door must have taken a long time because I fell asleep once again. In this realm it was very clear when I was awake and when I was asleep, meaning this was not a dream. When he finally reached the door, I was awakened by the sound of his hand jiggling the doorknob. I looked in that direction and with his hands on the doorknob he turned back to look at me. In that very moment as his head turned to look back at me, a black entity rushed from his body onto mine. This black spirit seemed to paralyze the entire left side of my body. There was a knowing that is hard to explain, but somehow, I knew that I was only paralyzed on one side. The right side of my body was fully mobile.

As this powerful, heavy spiritual force sat on one half of my body, internally I asked the question, "Is this real?" No sooner than my mind finished the question, the spiritual entity grabbed me under the arm, and I could feel what felt like fingers under my armpit. It pulled me closer and leaned into me, and in my ear said "Bri, no." It seemed to be warning me and telling me not to do something. Those were the only words it spoke. It was confusing because although the spiritual entity was dark and powerful it didn't seem to want to harm me.

Being raised in the Christian church, the only thing I knew to do was plead the Blood of Jesus, which is something Christians are taught to do to protect themselves and their families from harm or danger. I tried to get the words out of my mouth. I said, "The Blood of Jesus." Initially, I could not get it out because half of my mouth could not move. The entire left side of my body was completely paralyzed. I tried again to no avail. I kept trying to push the words, "The Blood of Jesus" out until finally on the fifth or sixth attempt. This spirit lifted itself off of my body and flew away.

I have no idea what this was. Although the entity's aura seemed dark, it appeared to be warning me or possibly even trying to help me. After discussing this with my good friend Kessan, she gave me a different perspective to consider. She suggests that the spirit saying "Bri no" was the spirit telling me not to plead the blood of Jesus because he knew he would have to flee if I continued. At one point I had convinced myself that D'Ablo was possessed by the sexual spirit of an "Incubus." During sex he would constantly ask me for full submission.

The message I *did* receive was clear, whether it was a warning, an awakening, or a message from another realm, I may never know. This connection was draining me spiritually. This connection was blocking my alignment. This connection was not my future and my soul was tired. That night taught me something I never forgot:

The body may crave what the soul rejects. Every time I tried to leave, the sexual connection pulled me back. Every time I tried to move forward, the soul tie tightened. Every time I tried to evolve, the connection tried to keep me the same. That is the danger of spiritual entanglement without spiritual alignment. A soul tie can feel like love but still be misaligned. A strong sexual bond does not guarantee a healthy emotional or spiritual bond. A divine lesson is not the same thing as a divine partner. He was my mountain — a spiritual obstacle I had to climb until I finally learned the lesson. And the lesson was this: You cannot attract a spiritually aligned partner while holding onto a spiritually misaligned one. The universe cannot bless clutter. God cannot move in confusion. Your person cannot enter a space already occupied by your toxic lover.

The Spiritual Psychology of Attraction

Studies show that 70% of people repeatedly attract the same type of partner because their nervous system is conditioned to choose familiarity over safety. You don't choose what you *want* —you choose what your wounds recognize.

When you heal, your attraction changes. Peace becomes attractive. Respect becomes non-negotiable. Consistency becomes sexy and emotional intelligence becomes magnetic. Spiritual depth becomes necessary. You begin attracting people who feel like oxygen, not chaos. That's why healing isn't just self-care —healing is spiritual preparation for aligned love.

Why Most People Struggle to Release Misaligned Lovers

People who love deeply often struggle to let go, not because they're weak, but because they're spiritually loyal. Your love is anchored in hope — the hope that your mate will rise into the version of themselves you see inside them.

But here's the truth:

You cannot climb into a person's soul and fix what they refuse to face.

You cannot force growth on someone who clings to stagnation.

You cannot wait your life away hoping someone will evolve.

And you cannot attract the mate God chose for you while entertaining the person your wounds chose for you.

How to Attract the Spiritually Aligned Partner You Deserve

Attracting a spiritually aligned partner isn't about looking outward — it's about elevating inward. You attract alignment when you become aligned.

You attract a spiritually grounded mate when you embody emotional stability.

You attract an open-hearted man or woman when you express your own truth.

You attract a kind person when you practice compassion.

You attract an evolved person when you continue your evolution.

You attract a partner who honors you when you honor yourself.

A spiritually aligned partner will not:

- drain your energy
- play with your emotions
- withhold love
- punish your confidence
- confuse your intuition

A spiritually aligned partner will:

- support your purpose
- meet you emotionally
- match your growth
- communicate clearly
- love gently
- elevate your spirit
- honor your body

· protect your peace

Alignment is not about perfection — it's about resonance.

Your Aligned Partner Is Still Coming

Somewhere in this world is a man or woman whose spirit matches yours. A person who:

· is kind by nature
· thinks deeply
· seeks truth
· loves without fear
· honors your sensitivity
· supports your purpose
· speaks your spiritual language
· explores the sacred and sexual connection with you
· meets your mind, your heart, your body, and your soul

You deserve a man or woman who awakens you, not wounds you. Who grows with you, not against you. Who sees your spirit, not just your beauty. Who chooses you intentionally, not conveniently. Your aligned partner will not feel like a mountain. They will feel like a meadow — peaceful, open, expansive, rooted, safe. You're not waiting on them. You're preparing for them. And they is preparing for you.

5

Conscious Love: Staying Connected After the Chemistry Fades

Falling in love is easy. It always has been. It's the rush, the spark, the butterflies, the late-night conversations, the electric pull of two bodies that cannot get enough of each other. It's the chemistry — that wild, intoxicating force that makes you feel like you've finally found someone who speaks the same invisible language as your soul.

But chemistry, no matter how powerful, is not connection. Chemistry ignites the relationship but conscious love sustains it, and that part — the sustaining — is where most relationships break. Not because the love wasn't real, but because the lovers were never taught the truth. Chemistry can start a fire, but only consciousness can keep it burning. The real test of love begins after the spark settles. After the "newness" fades. After the butterflies calm down. After you realize the person you adore is not magic — they're human. And so are you.

The Shift Nobody Talks About

People romanticize the beginning of love but rarely talk about what comes after. Not the ending — the middle. The quiet part. The part where you already know their smile, their scent, their laugh, their habits. The part where the high mellows out and you can finally see them without the thrill blinding you.

This is the place where real love begins.

Because the truth is this:

Chemistry is the universe introducing you.

Conscious love is the universe asking, "Now what will you do with this?"

That question separates infatuation from intimacy.

It separates passion from partnership.

It separates falling in love from staying in love.

When the spark softens, something sacred happens — the opportunity to actually *build* something with someone. Something real. Something grounded. Something intentional. Something that can hold both your shadows and your light.

Love Requires More Than the Beginning

It's easy to love someone when they're new.

It's easy to love someone when desire is high.

It's easy to love someone you barely know.

But love becomes conscious when:

- you stay when the novelty fades
- you reach for each other during quiet seasons
- you keep showing up during misunderstandings
- you discover deeper layers of each other

41

- you choose patience over pride
- you choose curiosity over assumptions
- you choose the relationship over your ego

Love becomes conscious when you realize:
**"I don't just want the spark —
I want the soul."**

The Quiet Beauty of the Middle

Nobody celebrates the middle stage of love, but it's where the sweetness actually lives.

It's in the ordinary moments:

- morning tea together
- inside jokes
- soft conversations on the couch
- the comfort of being fully seen
- the calm of someone who knows your patterns
- the trust that grows when passion no longer has to perform
- the peace that comes when you stop trying to impress one another

When chemistry fades, what remains is the truth of the connection — the emotional and spiritual thread that ties two souls together without the need for fireworks. Fireworks are beautiful, but they're temporary. A steady flame warms the whole house.

The Courage to Keep Choosing Love

The couples who last aren't the ones who never lost their spark — they're the ones who learned how to relight it. Together. With intention. With patience. With tenderness.

Conscious love says:

"I choose you in the slow seasons too."

"I choose you even when we don't see eye to eye."

"I choose you when it's work, not just pleasure."

"I choose you because something deeper than desire lives between us."

Chemistry is effortless.

Connection takes courage.

When the Mirror Appears

The longer you love someone, the more they become a mirror. Not just a mirror of your beauty — but of your wounds, your insecurities, your patterns, your triggers. This is why many relationships fall apart when the chemistry fades; when there is no spark to hide behind, the real you rises.

Conscious love is not scared of this part.

Conscious love says:

"Show me your truth.

Show me your fears.

Show me the parts you've kept hidden.

I'm not here to run — I'm here to understand."

Love without consciousness feels like pressure.

Love with consciousness feels like freedom.

Passion Can Return — but It Returns Differently

People think the loss of chemistry means the love is dying, but in reality, the spark often comes back — not as a wild flame, but as something deeper, slower, and richer.

Passion returns when you:

- rediscover each other
- speak openly
- create emotionally safe spaces
- learn new ways to connect
- laugh together
- heal individually
- grow spiritually
- stay curious

Chemistry returns when you create the conditions for it to rise again — not when you chase the version of each other you were in the first month.

And here's the truth most people never learn:

Conscious love brings a different kind of passion — one that feels like home, not chaos.

A Love That Doesn't Leave

The kind of love you're seeking isn't held together by butterflies — it's held together by intention.

It's held together by:

- honesty
- consistency

- emotional presence
- patience
- desire that matures into devotion
- two people who refuse to give up on each other

It's not about never losing the spark —

it's about never losing each other.

The real beauty of conscious love is this:

It doesn't depend on excitement to survive.

It depends on connection.

Two souls devoted.

Two spirits aligned.

Two humans choosing each other again and again.

Even on the days when life feels heavy.

Even on the days when desire is quiet.

Even when the chemistry softens and the real work begins.

What You Deserve

You deserve a love that stays after the chemistry fades.

A love that wants your soul, not just your curves.

A love that reaches for you even in silence.

A love that sees who you're becoming, not just who you were.

A love that deepens instead of disappearing.

A love that remembers how to touch your heart when life is touching your mind.

A love that chooses you consciously — not conveniently.

A love that lasts because it is intentional, sacred, patient, human, and divine.

You deserve the kind of love that doesn't need fireworks to know it's blessed.

A love that grows even in quiet seasons.

A love that becomes more beautiful with time.

A love that turns two healed, awakened souls into one aligned, extraordinary partnership. The chemistry may fade — but conscious love? That's where the real magic lives.

6

Soul Contracts, Karmic Ties & Twin Flames

There are people who walk into your life and feel strangely familiar — as if you've known them long before you ever met. People whose energy hits before their presence does, whose voice feels like déjà vu, whose eyes look like memory. You don't know why, and you can't explain it, but something pulls you toward them. Something deep. Something ancient. Something spiritual.

These are not everyday connections. These are soul contracts. These are karmic ties. These are twin flames. These are the people who change the trajectory of your life. They are the teachers disguised as lovers. The mirrors disguised as lessons. The disruptions disguised as destiny and if you're not grounded, awake, and spiritually aware, these connections can feel intoxicating, confusing, magnetic, painful, unforgettable — all at once. I learned this truth the hard way.

When Spiritual Hunger Makes You Vulnerable

When you're on a spiritual journey, you attract many voices — teachers, coaches, advisors, healers, gurus — and not all of them are aligned with truth. Some are sincere. Some are confused. And some are manipulative individuals who use spirituality as a mask to cover their human wounds.

I once had a life coach — a spiritual advisor — who insisted that in order for mankind to evolve, we must "transcend human emotion." According to him, emotions like sadness, pain, jealousy, fear, and grief were signs of spiritual immaturity. In his eyes, evolved beings feel nothing. They float above suffering, detached and enlightened.

At first, I believed him. I was desperate for healing. Desperate for answers. Desperate for release from the pain that had lived in my body since the day I witnessed my grandmother — the woman who raised me — die from a gunshot wound to the head. I was seventeen years old when I saw that. Seventeen. And for decades, that memory followed me like a shadow that never left.

So when this "master teacher" one who had mastered all the Laws of Maat, told me he had the key to erase that trauma forever, I clung to his words as if they came straight from God.

His name was **D-Amen Amere** — or at least that's what he called himself. He stood tall, dark-skinned, bald, and muscular and he carried himself like a prophet who had climbed spiritual mountains no one else could reach. He was a handsome, muscular black man. He assured me he had ascended beyond ordinary consciousness. He promised to take me through past-life regressions, guided meditations, and mystical exercises that would finally free me from my grandmother's death. He said he had been sent to me. He said we had been connected in past

48

lives, several incarnations together according to him. He told me I was chosen — and he was my spiritual key. And because I was hurting... I believed him.

When Healing Turns into Manipulation

Every week in his class I was told not to feel emotions. Not to cry or express fear. Not to acknowledge pain. Not to acknowledge him and other women. To him, emotions were "low vibration." He told me true spiritual masters feel nothing. But something in my spirit whispered, *This is not right.* Yet I stayed, because broken hearts follow whoever promises healing.

He and I began spending time together outside the spiritual center. We meditated privately. We read together. We worked out and trained together. We even meditated together.

Eventually, he convinced me that our connection was more than teacher and student — that it was divine, destined, pre-written. He said we were twin flames in multiple lifetimes. He told me his relationship with the woman he lived with was a mistake, that their connection wasn't spiritual, that he was meant for me and subconsciously he had moved from Texas to California for me even though we had not met yet.

And because I was spiritually hungry, emotionally wounded, and seeking relief from years of trauma... I believed him. I bought it all , hook-line and sinker.

Instead of healing, I was being spiritually seduced but I truly didn't understand that.

Experts in spiritual psychology warn that unhealed seekers are prime targets for manipulation. Dr. Clarissa Pinkola Estés, author of *Women Who Run With the Wolves*, writes:

"When a woman is searching for healing, she is in her most vulnerable state.

It is here that she must be most careful of those who claim to have the key to her soul."

I didn't know this at the time. But I know it now.

The Power I Forgot You Had

At that stage of my life, I didn't yet realize the truth:
No human being can heal you.
Only **YOU** — through God's grace — can do that.
Yet I handed him the authority over my healing.

I gave him access to my trauma. I gave him my trust. I gave him my vulnerability and he used every piece of it. When he became physically involved with me, I didn't resist or question it. I didn't think for one moment that anything was wrong. He had convinced me that our "spiritual bond" made intimacy necessary — part of our ascension, part of our past-life agreement, part of our twin flame destiny.

That's how soul ties form. Not always through love. Sometimes through wounds. Not always through truth. Sometimes through longing. Not always through alignment.Sometimes through manipulation.

Eventually, his inappropriate relationship with me violated the rules of the spiritual center where he taught, and they suspended him. The organization acted quickly and responsibly — but I was left with the emotional aftermath. I had to pick up the pieces he shattered. I had to face the pain of realizing I put my healing in the wrong hands. I had to accept that I gave my power to a man who only pretended to be a healer. I had to confront the truth that I hadn't yet learned: **You cannot outsource your healing. You must become your own healer.** And so, I did.

What Experts Say About Soul Ties, Karmic Bonds & Twin Flames

To understand why I fell so deeply into this connection — and why it took so long to let go — I had to learn about soul ties through a spiritual and psychological lens.

Soul Ties (Spiritual & Emotional Bonds)

Soul ties form through:

- deep emotional vulnerability
- sexual connection
- trauma bonding
- spiritual manipulation
- shared wounds

Dr. Caroline Myss, world-renowned spiritual teacher, explains:

> *"A soul tie happens when two people exchange energetic fragments of themselves.*
> *The deeper the emotional or physical connection, the deeper the tie."*

Some soul ties are healthy.
  Most are lessons.

Mine was a lesson.

Karmic Ties (Past-Life or Ancestral Contracts)

Karmic relationships are not meant to last.
 They are meant to teach.
 They reveal:

- patterns you need to break
- wounds you need to heal
- boundaries you need to develop
- cycles you must end

A karmic partner often feels irresistible — but unstable.
 Experts say the strongest karmic ties often come with:

- intense attraction
- emotional highs and lows
- confusion
- a feeling of "destiny" mixed with turmoil

That was exactly what happened with D-Amen.

Twin Flames (Mirror Souls)

The twin flame concept is beautiful — but misunderstood.
 A true twin flame does not manipulate.
 A true twin flame does not abuse your vulnerability.
 A true twin flame does not block your healing or spiritual evolution.
 Twin flame "runners" and "chasers" are often trauma re-

sponses, not divine destiny.

Spiritual psychologist Jeff Brown says:

> *"Many relationships labeled 'twin flames' are trauma bonds in disguise."*

This man was not my twin flame or my soul mate.

He was a karmic lesson.

A spiritual mirror.

An emotional teacher.

He showed me the parts of myself that still needed healing.

He revealed the wounds I had ignored.

He reflected my vulnerability back to me.

And most importantly:

He forced me to reclaim my own power.

The Moment I Took My Power Back

After everything fell apart, I realized the most important truth of all:

God already gave me the tools to heal. I was the one who needed to use them. So I turned inward. I meditated deeper and I sat in silence longer. I studied myself. I confronted my patterns and I learned emotional responsibility and self-awareness. I learned to stop searching for saviors. I learned that my soul is my responsibility and no human being can heal me.

That painful chapter opened the door to the greatest spiritual awakening of my life: I am my own healer. Go has already given me the power. I am my own guide. I am my own key. And once I accepted that, everything changed.

What That Connection Taught Me

He taught me:

- to trust my intuition
- to stop ignoring red flags
- to stop letting others define my spirituality
- to recognize spiritual manipulation
- to question anyone who claims divine authority
- to always listen to my emotional truth
- to never abandon myself again
- to never mistake intensity for alignment

And most importantly:

I learned that not every soul that enters your life is meant to stay.

Some come to awaken you.

Some come to break you open.

Some come to teach you who you really are.

He was not my destiny.

He was my lesson.

Soul Contracts Are Not Always Romantic — But They Are Always Transformational

I no longer regret meeting him and I do not resent the experience. I no longer shame myself for falling for his spiritual persona. I now see the connection for what it truly was:

A soul contract designed to lead me back to myself.

Some soul contracts feel like blessings.

Some feel like heartbreak.

Some feel like confusion.
Some feel like fire.
But all soul contracts lead you to evolution.

You Are Your Own Divine Connection

We may come across many teachers in this lifetime — some genuine, some wounded, some deceptive. But the greatest teacher will always be the one within you. The soul tie with D-Amen did not break me. It broke me **open**. It pushed me deeper into my spiritual journey. It awakened truths I had been ignoring. It reminded me that God placed all healing power inside me — not inside any man. And as painful as the chapter was, it brought me to a place of self-love, self-trust, and spiritual clarity that I had been searching for my entire life.

I am grateful for the lesson. Grateful for the awakening. Grateful for the evolution. And now I know this with absolute certainty: **Your soul will deliver you to the right people for the right reasons — but it will also deliver you to the wrong people for the right lessons.**
Every tie teaches you something. Every bond has a purpose. Every connection has a message. Some prepare you. Some stretch you. Some break you open so God can rebuild you stronger. This was mine. And now... I am ready for the aligned love that was always meant to find me and I pray it finds each and every one of you too.

7

When the Spirit Speaks: The Body as a Divine Messenger

I have always believed that God speaks to us in different ways — through intuition, signs, synchronicities, dreams, sudden clarity, or even the quiet knowing that rises from deep within. But over the years, I discovered something about myself that once confused me, then frightened me, and now finally makes sense: my body reacts to the presence of divine truth.

Not metaphorically.

Not symbolically.

Physically.

There is something about being in the air — somewhere between heaven and earth — that opens a channel inside me. As if my spirit becomes lighter the moment the wheels leave the ground. As if altitude removes interference and tunes me directly into the frequency of God.

I don't fully understand it, but I know this: I am closest to the Divine Source when I'm flying. Up there, inspiration hits me like waves. Thoughts untangle themselves. Ideas download effortlessly. Problems resolve without effort. Clarity floods my mind like sunlight pouring into a dark room.

I've written entire chapters in the sky — including pieces of my best selling book *Your Mind is Magic.* One day on a flight home from Bali, Indonesia something happened to me at 30,000 feet. Something beyond logic. Something that felt like spiritual electricity running through my veins.

The Day My Body Reacted to God

One of the most powerful spiritual moments of my life happened on a plane returning from Bali, Indonesia — a sacred trip, a spiritual retreat with some amazing women from different parts of the world. This incident opened my heart in ways I didn't expect.

I remember settling into an empty row. Halfway through the flight, an overwhelming presence overcame me. It was stronger than anything I had ever felt. My body started reacting before my mind could even process what was happening.

I felt every emotion and its opposite all at once:

I felt the urge to cry, the urge to laugh.

I felt joy, then sorrow.

I felt peace, then I started trembling.

I felt heat... an intensity rising in my chest.

I felt **sexual arousal**.

My body began to twitch lightly — not in fear, but in recognition. As if something holy was moving through me, rearranging things I didn't even know were out of place.

I felt grateful no one was sitting beside me, because had they been there, they might have thought something was wrong. But nothing was wrong. **Everything was right.**

I felt a pull — not emotional, not mental, but spiritual — to

57

write.

I didn't have a journal, but I had the book I had been reading on the flight: *The Law of Attraction: How To Get What You Want* by Robert Collier. With nowhere else to put the words rushing out of me, I turned to the blank back pages of that book, and then... it happened.

I always describe the next part this way: **Something came through me.** Not around me. Not beside me. Through me.

As a seasoned speaker and Toastmasters member, I'm familiar with expressive language. But the words that spilled out of me felt foreign — not unfamiliar, but higher. Wiser. Older than me. Like they belonged to something ancient.

This is what I wrote in the back of that book:

"The separation of religions are distractions.
We are all one, infinitely connected to the Divine Source.
One God for us all.
He lies within the Christian, the Buddhist, the Hindu equally.
Our desires are like sunlight. They are inexhaustible.
You can just as easily taste of the sweet fruit as you can the bitter. You choose.
Most of mankind is on the wrong path — a path of separation and distinction from each other. Great unnecessary energy is wasted in proving these non-existent differences.
Your brother, your sister, and all of mankind deserve equal blessing from God, but have received them in unequal portions because inequality is believed to be a truth even for oneself.
Punishment from God is a fabrication of man.

God is love."

When I read it back, I didn't recognize it as my own writing. Yes, the ideas reflected my beliefs — but the tone, the voice, the depth... it felt like something was delivering a message **through** me, not *from* me. At that moment I knew that this was confirmation. This was alignment. **This was God speaking through my body.** I'm certain of it.

When Spiritual Energy Awakens the Physical Body

For years, I tried to understand why I react so strongly to spiritual truth. Why goosebumps, tears, trembling — and yes, at times even **sexual arousal** — rise when I encounter divine knowledge. It used to embarrass me. I used to hide it. I didn't know how to explain it to anyone. Until I learned that I am not alone.

Many spiritual practitioners — including mystics, Kundalini teachers, yogis, monks, and even neuroscientists — have documented the same phenomenon.

They call it:

- Kundalini activation
- Energetic awakening
- Sacred body response
- Somatic spiritual release
- Divine resonance

In ancient spiritual texts, it's said that when divine truth is present, the body becomes a vessel that cannot hide its recognition.

Dr. Andrew Newberg, a neuroscientist known for studying spiritual experiences, writes:

> *"When a person encounters profound spiritual truth, the brain activates the same pleasure and reward centers stimulated during deep love or intense emotional experience."*

This is why:

- some weep during prayer
- some shiver during meditation
- some feel heat rise up their spine
- some feel energy move in the lower chakras
- some twitch, shake, or tremble
- some feel arousal — not sexual, but **spiritual**

It is not inappropriate.
It is not sinful.
It is not embarrassing.
It is divine physiology.
It is the soul recognizing something
that the body cannot deny.

Why It Happened to Me on That Plane

I wasn't:

- hallucinating
- imagining
- overwhelmed

- emotional
- stressed

I was **open**.

Airplanes create the perfect conditions for spiritual alignment:

- stillness
- altitude
- separation from earthly noise
- uninterrupted silence
- contemplative space
- bodily relaxation
- liminal energy between worlds

I was suspended above the world — literally and spiritually.

And in that openness, God spoke. Through feeling and through emotion. Through the physical body. That arousal I once felt reading spiritual material? It was the same phenomenon. The same energetic awakening. The same divine channel opening. The same sacred frequency rising through my physical self. My body was saying: "Pay attention." My spirit was saying: "This is alignment. This is Divine connection." God was saying: "This is Me."

Many people have spiritual gifts, but I want everyone reading this to know: That your sensitivity is not a weakness — it is your gift. There are people who spend their entire lives numb to spiritual energy. But some can feel it — in their mind, their emotions, and in their body. Their spiritual channel is **somatic** — a living, breathing instrument God uses to communicate through sensation. Your sensitivity is **part of your calling.** It is not something to hide or tone down. It is the mechanism God uses to speak to you, guide you, protect you, and awaken you.

Do not let people tell you that you are:

- "too emotional"
- "too intense"
- "too sensitive"
- "too much"

Many of us are **spiritually gifted** — and our body feels what our soul already knows. If there is one truth I want you to carry from this chapter, it is this: Your body is not separate from your spirit. Your sexuality is not separate from your divinity. Your sensitivity is not separate from your purpose.

Every flutter you feel during prayer, every chill that runs across your skin when truth enters the room, every tear, every tremble, every warm surge in your chest or below it — none of it is shameful. It is sacred. It is your soul confirming what your mind cannot yet explain.

You were not created to be numb. You were not created to disconnect from your body. You were not created to silence your desire. Your passion is a gift. Your intuition is a compass. Your sensitivity is a language. Your spiritual and sensual energies are two rivers flowing from the same Divine Source and no matter your identity, your orientation, your background, or your path —**you deserve to feel whole inside your own skin.**

So let this be your permission, to feel deeply. To sense truth. To embrace your sexual energy without shame. To honor your spiritual gifts without fear. To trust the signals your body sends to you. Because the same God who speaks through visions and dreams also speaks through the body. And every time your heart pounds, or your breath is taken away in awe, your skin tingles, or your spirit rises....you are to remember that you are a phenomenal creation of God. He designed you perfectly. He did not make any mistakes, so love yourself and honor all of your feelings.

8

Love as a Spiritual Frequency

Most people talk about love like it's an event. A meeting. A kiss. A relationship or a moment in time when two people collide and suddenly everything feels magical and right. But love is not an event — **love is a frequency.** It is a vibration that lives inside the body, moves through the spirit, and radiates outward into the world long before another person ever arrives.

If you are not vibrating at the frequency of love, you will not recognize it even when it's standing right in front of you. I learned that the hard way. For years, I thought love was something you *earned* through sacrifice, something you had to fight to keep, something you gave until you had nothing left, something you endured until someone finally saw your worth. I used to believe love was the outcome of effort, loyalty, pain, patience, or timing.

But real love — the divine kind, the aligned kind, the soul-level kind —does not come from effort. It comes from frequency. The love that elevates you is not created by the relationship. It is created by the vibration you hold long before you meet anyone.

And the more spiritually awake I became, the more I understood that **love is not something you fall into — it's something you rise into.**

Love Begins in the Spirit Before It Breathes in the Body

People often say, "I'll love fully when I meet the right partner." But that's not how frequency works. You don't wait until someone arrives to start vibrating at love — you become love itself, and the frequency of love attracts its match. Like attract like.

I didn't always understand this. I spent years trying to "love right" from a wounded place:

- loving men who weren't aligned
- forgiving what should have been boundaries
- hoping my compassion would heal someone else's trauma
- staying loyal to connections God never assigned to me
- confusing chemistry with destiny
- calling karmic ties "soul mates"
- mistaking intensity for spiritual meaning

And in all of that, I didn't realize that my internal lower vibration was choosing my partners for me. Wounded women attract wounded men and visa versa. Unhealed hearts attract unhealed love. Confused souls attract chaotic connections. Because frequency is law.You cannot vibrate at fear and receive love. You cannot vibrate at loneliness and receive partnership. You cannot vibrate at insecurity and receive devotion. You cannot vibrate at chaos and receive peace. Love always follows vibration.

There Are Levels to the Frequency of Love

There is:

Human love — emotional and fragile.

Love based on feelings, physical connection, attachment, and circumstance. This kind of love changes. It rises and falls. It depends on mood, conversation, behavior, and attraction. Then there is:

Soul love — ancient, familiar, magnetic.

This is the love I wrote about in Chapter 6.

The kind I felt with my first and second husband.

The kind that feels predestined, powerful, irresistible.

But soul love is not always aligned love.

Sometimes it's just karmic energy completing its cycle.

And finally, there is:

Divine love — the highest frequency.

The love that meets you at the level of your evolution.

The love that honors your spirit.

The love that feels like God's breath on your life.

The love that requires consciousness, healing, truth, and spiritual maturity.

Divine love is not chaotic.

Divine love is not confusing.

Divine love is not conditional.

Divine love doesn't break you down —

it awakens you.

This is the frequency we are all trying to reach, even when we don't know that's what we're doing.

Our Body Knows the Frequency of Love Before Your Mind Does

We all have a gift **our body recognizes truth in many ways:**

It shakes.

It trembles.

It heats.

It cries.

It laughs.

It tingles.

It awakens.

It releases.

It reacts.

It reacts because love is not just emotional —it is energetic.

When we feel divine presence so strongly our bodies definitely respond. Remember that our body is not separate from our soul — it is the messenger of it. In mystical traditions, they call this:

· **Kundalini rising**
· **spiritual ecstasy**
· **ori awakening**
· **divine resonance**
· **somatic enlightenment**

But you don't need anyone else's terminology. You know what it is...instinctively, subconsciously. We All Know!

Love Is the Highest Spiritual Technology

Love rearranges the nervous system. It softens trauma stored in the bones. It rewrites emotional memory. It restores belief. It heightens intuition. It expands consciousness. It aligns the heart with purpose. It heals wounds that therapy can't reach. It dissolves illusions. It awakens destiny. The frequency of love is the closest vibration to the Divine Source. That's why our bodies react to spiritual truth — truth is love. God is love. Healing is love. Awakening is love and when you encounter pure love — not emotional love, but **energetic love** — your entire being rises.

What Happens When You Raise Your Love Frequency

When you elevate your frequency to love, you attract different experiences: You stop desiring what drains you. You stop loving from emptiness. You stop accepting inconsistent affection. You stop mistaking intensity for intimacy. You stop confusing chemistry with compatibility. You stop revisiting men who do not value you. You stop entertaining low-vibration partnerships. Instead, you become magnetic to:

- emotionally mature men & women
- spiritually awakened partners
- peaceful relationships
- healthy communication
- devotion
- presence
- intentional love
- consistency
- depth

- kindness
- spiritual connection
- mutual respect

Our true nature is love and love as a frequency can change your entire life. It doesn't just bring you a partner — it brings you ALIGNMENT.

You Don't Find Love — You Become It

People think finding love is a search on Pof or Tender. But love is not something you find. Love is something you **become**. When you vibrate at the frequency of love, you don't chase anything. You attract everything. You magnetize what matches your spirit.

Your partner — your real partner — will show up when your frequency becomes the home their soul recognizes. Because love, in its highest form, is not a feeling. It is not an emotion. It is not luck. **Love is a spiritual frequency** — the highest one —and when you hold it, everything meant for you shows up in your life.

9

The Tao of Love and Alignment**

When I first discovered the *Tao Te Ching*, I didn't fully under-stand it. Lao Tzu's words were simple, quiet, soft — but layered with a depth that only reveals itself when your spirit is ready to receive it. And that's exactly how divine wisdom works: it arrives gently, but transforms everything it touches.

The Tao — pronounced "Dow" — is an ancient Chinese philosophy that literally means **The Way.**

Not the way of religion.

Not the way of rules.

Not the way of force.

The Way of alignment.

The Way of flow.

The Way of allowing.

The Way of inner peace.

And the more spiritually awakened I became, the more I realized how deeply the Tao aligned with my own journey — especially the journey of love, embodiment, sexuality, and spiritual frequency.

It teaches that life is not supposed to be forced. Love is not supposed to be chased. Healing is not supposed to be pressured. Alignment is not supposed to be pushed. Everything you are meant to experience unfolds with ease when you stop resisting who you truly are.

Wayne Dyer — one of my favorite spiritual teachers — said it best:

> "When you change the way you look at things, the things you look at change."

But the Tao took it even further:

When you change the way you *vibrate*, the things you attract change.

The Tao is not about doing. It is about *being*. And love — real love — begins with being.

The First Lesson of the Tao: Stop Forcing, Start Allowing

The Tao teaches that nothing in nature struggles to be what it is. Water doesn't try to flow.....it just flows. The sun doesn't try to shine....it simply shines. Grass doesn't try to grow, it grows because that is its nature. If a river encounters a rock, it doesn't attack it. It doesn't get angry. It doesn't try to break the rock. It doesn't question its worth. It doesn't wonder if it's good enough. Water simply moves around the obstacle — softly, effortlessly, wisely — and continues its journey.

That is the Tao. That is the Way. That is alignment. And that is what love should feel like. We have all forced something that wasn't meant for us — a partner, a relationship, a connection, a version of ourselves we thought we had to become in order to be loved.

But the Tao whispers: **"What is meant for you flows to you. What is not meant for you will drain you."** When you are aligned with yourself, you don't chase love — you allow it.

The Second Lesson: Softness Is Strength

In the Tao Te Ching, Lao Tzu writes:

"The softest thing in the world overcomes the hardest."

This wasn't just philosophy — this was revelation. For so long, I believed strength meant being unbreakable. I believed strength meant never showing weakness. I believed strength meant carrying everything alone. I had suffered through so much in my younger years, I believed strength meant staying hard to survive. i prided myself on being a tough Leo woman.

But softness — true softness — is divine strength. Softness is staying open after being hurt. Softness is still loving after heartbreak. Softness is trusting your intuition. Softness is flowing instead of forcing. Softness is allowing instead of controlling. Softness is choosing peace over validation. Softness is choosing alignment over ego. Love is a soft energy, not a hard one. Healing is a soft energy. Spirituality is a soft energy. God is a soft energy. The Tao teaches that everything powerful is soft at first — even light.

The Third Lesson: Wholeness Attracts Wholeness

Wayne Dyer often taught that:

> *"You cannot give away what you do not have."*

If you want love, you must *be* love. If you want peace, you must *cultivate* peace. If you want alignment, you must *embody* alignment. The Tao supports this by teaching that: **You attract what you are, not what you desire.** This has shown up in every chapter of my life:

- When I was wounded, I attracted wounded love.
- When I was uncertain, I attracted men who were emotionally unavailable.
- When I was spiritually hungry, I attracted false teachers.
- When I was healing, I attracted karmic ties that brought lessons.
- When I became aligned, I attracted peace and clarity.

I'm in no rush now. I know now that when I'm ready, I have the power with-in me to manifest the perfect mate for me, and so you all of you.

Love, like the Tao, is not an external hunt — it is an internal beautiful frequency. The more whole you become, the more whole your relationships become.

The Fourth Lesson: The Uncarved Block

One of my favorite Taoist concepts is the *uncarved block* — the idea that we are born whole, pure, untouched, perfect. And that life cuts into us, creating what I call *Holes* formed from trauma, childhood, religion, heartbreak, expectations, death, rejection, societal rules. Theses traumas create holes in our hearts that get bigger with each new painful situation. These incidents carve away pieces of our original truth. We try to live our lives anyway with these gaping holes. Unfortunately we hurt others along the way. We spend a life time searching for all those small broken pieces of our hearts trying to put ourselves back together again. But the Tao teaches us to return to our natural state too undo the carvings. To mend the holes, to unlearn the conditioning. To love ourselves and come back home to who we truly are, and that is pure love.

This resonates with my journey so deeply — from trauma, to strict religious doctrine, to spiritual awakening, to personal evolution. Every chapter of my life has been a mending and a uncarving. In so grateful that i have lived ling enough for those holes to begin closing. Healing is possible. We do not have to allow things that happen to us in our past to affect our lives forever.

Love is easiest to receive when you return to your uncarved self — the version of you that existed before the world hurt you. The Tao reminds us that we don't heal by becoming something new — we heal by remembering who we were before the world changed us.

The Fifth Lesson: Nonresistance Creates Miracles

The Tao teaches that resistance is the root of suffering. Every time you resist what is, you disconnect from what could be. Resistance sounds like:

"This person *should* love me this way."

"This relationship *should* work."

"He *should* change."

"I *should* be over this by now."

"I *should* be further along in life"

"Life *shouldn't* be this hard."

All of these are battles against reality. All of these create spiritual friction. You have the free will to change anything in your life that you do not like.

Wayne Dyer said:

> *"There is no stress in the world — only people resisting the way things are."*

When you embrace the Tao, you stop resisting and start flowing. Love flows to you. Healing flows. Alignment flows. Happiness. Prosperity flows. Destiny flows. Everything you force becomes misaligned. Everything you allow becomes effortless.

How the Tao Applies to Love, Sexuality, and Your Spiritual Journey

The Tao is not just a philosophy — it's a lived experience.
It shows up when:

- your body reacts to spiritual truth
- you feel divine inspiration while flying
- your energy rises during meditation
- your intuition speaks louder than your logic
- your heart knows before your mind does
- love flows to you without effort
- misaligned connections fall away
- you attract partners who match your vibration
- you refuse to settle into anything that disrupts your peace

The Tao is the frequency of my entire book.
My writing itself is the Tao. My writing is Love.
It is soft, surrendered, intuitive, flowing, unforced, aligned.
I write not from the mind, but from my spirit.
And the Tao says:

"When you align with your true nature, everything you seek will come to you." Be it Love, connection, healing, purpose, peace, prosperity, awakening, divine partnership. All of it flows to those who flow with in Love and Peace.

The Tao Is the Highest Love Frequency

The Tao teaches:

- Be still.

- Be clear.
- Be true.
- Be present.
- Be open.
- Be peaceful.
- Be aligned.

And when you become that energy, you become a magnet. The universe responds. People respond. Love responds, God responds. There is no climbing, chasing, trying, begging, proving, or forcing. Only receiving.

The Tao is the quietest spiritual teaching — but it carries the loudest truth:

When you become aligned with the frequency of love, everything meant for you arrives without struggle.

And that is the lesson. That is the wisdom. That is The Way.

10

The Spiritual Lover

When most people hear the words *Kama Sutra*, their minds jump straight to sex positions. Western culture reduced one of the most profound spiritual texts in human history into a novelty handed out at bachelorette parties.

But the true meaning of the Kama Sutra — the original meaning — has very little to do with acrobatic sex and everything to do with awakened connection, self-knowledge, and sacred intimacy.

The Kama Sutra is not about performance. It is about **presence**. It is not about lust. It is about **consciousness**. It is not about the physical body. It is about the **energetic body**, the **emotional body**, and the **spiritual body** meeting in harmony.

The more I've grown in my own spiritual journey — the more I've understood my own body, my own sexual energy, and the inexplicable moments of divine arousal I've experienced — the more clearly I've seen why texts like the Kama Sutra were created in the first place.

It is a guide for people who understand that sexual energy

is spiritual energy. And when it is awakened consciously, it becomes a pathway to the Divine.

Kama: The Sanskrit Word That Western Culture Misunderstood

The word *Kama* does not simply mean "sex."

It means **desire, love, sensuality, connection, and pleasure aligned with spiritual truth.**

Desire *itself* is not sinful —the Hindu texts teach that desire is one of the four pillars of a complete, balanced, and spiritually meaningful life. They believed sexual energy is a life force, not a shameful secret.

So when the Kama Sutra speaks of intimacy, it is not teaching:

- how to seduce
- how to impress
- how to perform
- how to dominate
- how to be desirable

It is teaching:

How to become deeply present with your partner.

How to exchange energy consciously.

How to merge spiritually, not just physically.

How to awaken divine connection.

The text is only sexual on the surface.

Underneath, it is about the sacredness of union.

The Kama Sutra and the Connection to Your Body's Spiritual Reactions

I've shared openly — bravely — about the sacred moments when my body reacted to spiritual truth:

- the arousal that rose when you read something deeply divine
- the trembling and divinely-inspired writing on the plane
- the heat of spiritual presence moving through you
- the sudden bursts of emotion when truth came into your awareness

Those moments weren't random.

And they weren't inappropriate.

They were **Kama Sutra moments** — even if you didn't know it.

The Kama Sutra teaches that the body holds spiritual receptors.

That the body reacts when the soul recognizes something true.

That divine energy moves through the same channels as sexual energy.

In fact, ancient teachers believed:

> *"Spiritual bliss and sexual bliss are born from the same fire."*

The Kama Sutra Believed Your Body is a Spiritual Instrument

This is one of the core teachings of the text, but it was erased by Western interpretations. The Kama Sutra teaches that your body is:

- a channel
- a receiver
- a transmitter
- an instrument for divine experience

Your sexual energy is the **most direct path to spiritual awakening**, because it forces you to:

- be present
- surrender control
- open your heart
- feel deeply
- merge with another soul
- experience vulnerability
- release ego

Sexual energy is raw truth. And raw truth is spiritual. Your body *tells the truth before your mind does.* The Kama Sutra confirms exactly that.

Where Sexuality Meets God

In the West, people were taught: "Sex is sinful. Sex is dirty. Sex is something God disapproves of." But ancient spiritual traditions believed the opposite: Sex — when aligned with love, connection, and presence — becomes an act of worship. Not worship of the partner. Worship of the Divine energy flowing through both bodies. The Kama Sutra teaches that when two aligned souls join intimately:

- their breath synchronizes
- their hearts align
- their chakras open
- their energy fields merge
- their spirits rise
- their intuition strengthens
- their consciousness expands
- their souls remember each other

This is why sex can feel sacred. This is why it can feel addictive. This is why it can feel healing. This is why it can feel destabilizing with the wrong partner. This is why some people mistake sexual chemistry for destiny. Because **sexual energy is spiritual energy.** Always, not sometimes, not occasionally, not depending on the partner, but Always.

The Kama Sutra teaches the exact phenomenon I experienced on the plane and describes it as **the body remembering God.** That overwhelming wave of emotion I had — the laughing and crying simultaneously — that wasn't confusion. It was alignment. That involuntary twitching. It was energy moving. That urge to write what was coming through me. It was divine inspiration channeling through me.

The Kama Sutra says:
> *"When the mind is open and the heart is surrendered, the Divine moves through the body without resistance."*

That's exactly what happened to me at 30,000 feet. I now know my story is not strange, or as rare as I thought. It was ancient. It was sacred. It was beautiful. It was absolutely spiritual. I lived what the Kama Sutra teaches — without ever needing the book to explain it.

Sacred Sexuality Is Not About Sex — It's About Wholeness

The Kama Sutra is not a book about positions. It is a book about *presence* and it teaches:

- emotional vulnerability
- spiritual connection
- energetic understanding
- conscious intimacy
- sacred embodiment
- honoring your partner
- honoring yourself
- honoring the Divine within both of you

It is the meeting point of love, desire, spirituality, and truth. Sexuality is not separate from spirituality. It is one of the highest expressions of it.

I wrote this specific chapter because I want everyone reading to understand the importance of aligning with the higher frequency of love.

This chapter shows you that love is not just emotional — it is physical, mental, spiritual, energetic, and sacred. I want you all to understand:

- why your bodies react the way they do
- why sexual connections feel spiritually powerful
- why certain lovers feel like destiny
- why intimacy can heal or harm
- why divine love feels like both fire and peace
- why sexual frequency affects emotional well-being
- why spiritual awakening often comes with physical sensations

The Kama Sutra ties all of this together beautifully.

Sex is not the opposite of God. Sex is one of the languages of God and and when two individuals meet consciously, intentionally, spiritually, and energetically...Sex becomes a beautiful prayer. Touch becomes an intensive meditation. Desire becomes devotion. Union becomes awakening and Love becomes enlightenment.

That is the truth the Kama Sutra has tried to teach the world for thousands of years.

And now, you have been introduced to it.

11

11:11 — The Gateway to Alignment, Awakening & Sacred Union

There are moments in life when the universe speaks to us in numbers. Patterns. Signs. Symbols. Repetition that seems too intentional to ignore. And one of the most powerful signs — one that millions of people around the world have experienced — is the appearance of **11:11**.

For years, people have wondered what it means. Is it an angel number? A message from the universe? A whisper from a higher dimension? A sign of awakening? A calling A reminder?

I see this number continuously. I always stop and breathe and thank God. It makes me instantly feel gratitude for my life.

We many never understand why God speaks to us in signs and symbols. I have come to terms with not knowing WHY. I accept it and set my own intention to why these numerical numbers or angel numbers as some say, show up in my life. 11:11, 33, 55 , 222 etc have always felt like confirmation that there is a power greater than us. It's like a spiritual nudge, a soft tap on the shoulder, a moment when the universe asks: **"Are you paying**

attention?"

The Numerology of 11:11 — A Spiritual Portal

In numerology, **1** is the number of new beginnings.

A single spark.

A seed.

A thought.

A intention.

A desire forming.

When the number appears doubled — **11** — it becomes a sacred master number representing:

- intuition
- spiritual awakening
- alignment
- psychic insight
- divine connection
- the merging of two energies

Now look at **11:11** — a double alignment.

A mirrored frequency.

A spiritual echo.

11:11 is said to be a portal, a moment where the physical world and the spiritual world touch fingertips. People often see 11:11 when they're awakening spiritually. When they are healing. When they are remembering something ancient and divine inside themselves. The deeper your consciousness becomes, the more often you'll notice 11:11. Not because the number appears more — but because *you are finally aware enough to see it.*

Why 11:11 Shows Up During Emotional or Sexual Awakening

Here's what most people don't know: Spiritual awakening and sexual awakening often happen at the same time. Your sexual energy is your **life-force energy** — the same energy that awakens intuition, enhances creativity, opens spiritual channels, and elevates your consciousness.

And **11:11** often appears during moments of:

- emotional transformation
- deep healing
- spiritual surrender
- sexual alignment
- heightened intuition
- awakening of self

Because in those moments, your energy rises, and **11:11** mirrors that rise. **11:11** is the universe telling you: "Your vibration just shifted. You are awakening. You are remembering. Stay present."

The Twin Pillars: Why 11:11 Mirrors Relationship Energy

Look at the shape of **11:11**. Four vertical pillars. Two pairs. Two mirrors.

It represents:

- union
- partnership
- alignment

- reflection
- spiritual merging
- twin flame energy
- soul recognition

This is why many people begin seeing **11:11** when they meet (or release) a powerful soulmate or karmic partner. The number itself is a symbol of divine pairing.

It mirrors:

You + your higher self

You + your soulmate

You + your destiny

You + alignment

You + your spiritual path

It is a reminder that you are not walking alone —your soul, your guides, and the universe are communicating with you through synchronicity.

11:11 As a Sexual-Spiritual Signal

This is the part people rarely discuss, but it is truth: Sexual energy amplifies spiritual alignment and spiritual alignment amplifies sexual energy. When your energy rises — when your heart opens — when your intuition is activated — when your soul is present— when love becomes conscious —your sexual energy becomes more alive, more sacred, more felt, more connected.

This is why many people (not just me lol) have sensed arousal during spiritual downloads. Sexual energy recognizes divine truth. The body knows the frequency before your mind interprets it. In the spiritual world, this is known as:

- kundalini rising
- divine feminine awakening
- sacred sensuality
- shakti energy
- soul-body integration

The Kama Sutra hinted at it.

The Tao validated it. My plane experience confirms it. **11:11** is the synchronization of the body, mind, soul, and energy. A moment where everything aligns. A moment where God speaks through numbers. A moment where your entire being rises.

If you are seeing 11:11 often is a reminder that: You are guided. You are aligned. You are awakening. You are becoming who God created you to be. You are remembering and you are never alone on this life and that you are made in the image of God.

Everything you desire — love, sexuality, peace, happiness, spiritual connection — already lives within you. All you need to do is stay aligned. Continue to allow your thoughts to create your reality. Meditate, pray, plant your feet in the earth and ground yourself. Choose to smile and be kind to yourself and others and you will continue to evolve into you Higher Self.

About the Author

SaBrina Fisher Reece is a creative author, artist, and entrepreneur. Above all, she is a dedicated mother of four and a loving "Grammie" to two grandsons. She is passionate about making a positive impact on the world and is committed to sharing the transformative tools she has utilized in her own personal transformation

journey with future generations.

Her first book, *My Spiritual Smile: Tools for Mental and Emotional Transformation*, recounts her traumatic past and provides readers with the methods she used to heal from abandonment and childhood tragedy. Her second book, *Your Mind Is Magic*, which she considers her masterpiece, emphasizes that the mind is powerful and must be controlled, or it will control us. We have the power to master our thoughts and Manipulate Ideas in a New Positive Direction.

When SaBrina isn't writing self-help books, she is teaching sound meditation classes at A New Vision Studio in Los Angeles or giving dynamic motivational speeches to audiences of men, women, and children, reminding them that anything is possible if they believe in themselves. **@ SoundWithSaBrina www.Sound WithSaBrina.com**

You can connect with me on:

f https://www.facebook.com/author.sabrinareece.3

Also by SaBrina Fisher Reece

Daily practical tools on how to stay positive throughout the up's and downs of life

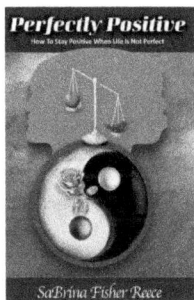

Perfectly Positive

erfectly Positive is your guide to staying centered, grounded, and hopeful in an imperfect world. Through real-life stories, practical tools, and soul-level wisdom, SaBrina Fisher Reece shows you how to rise above daily stress, disappointments, and negative thinking to create a life rooted in peace and purpose. This book teaches you how to master your thoughts, elevate your vibration, and choose a positive perspective—even when life isn't cooperating. Inspiring, relatable, and deeply transformative, *Perfectly Positive* reminds you that happiness is not found in perfection... it's created by the power of your own mind.